What Do I Say When I Pray?

A Handbook for Praying With Results

by Darlene Hoffa

STANDARD PUBLISHING
Cincinnati, Ohio   11-03017

Unless otherwise noted, all Scripture quotations are from the *Holy Bible: New International Version,* ©1973, 1978, 1984 by the International Bible Society. Used by permission of Zondervan Bible Publishers and the International Bible Society.

Library of Congress Cataloging in Publication Data:

Hoffa, Darlene.
      What do I say when I pray? : a handbook for praying with results /
   by Darlene Hoffa.
         p.   cm.
      ISBN 0-87403-667-4
      1. Prayer.   2. Prayer—Problems, exercises, etc.   I. Title.
   BV215.H63   1990
   248.3'2—dc20   s89-48889
                                                                            CIP

Cover photo ©COMSTOCK.

Contents

Introduction

"What a morning!" Karen said, as she rushed in to help Ginger, Lucy, and me finish the last mailing for a writers' conference. During preparations for the upcoming event, our friendship had flourished. Discussions ranged from writing projects to anticipated vacations.

"You know how Darlene is always telling us to pray specifically," Karen continued. "Just wait 'til you hear what I asked for this morning."

When no one interrupted, Karen continued, "Our Bible study group is holding a fifties party, and I volunteered to find trivia questions about music from that era. I decided to ask God to help me find them fast. This week I can't afford spending extra time looking for them."

Ginger snatched her purse from under the table. "You're not going to believe this," she gasped. Within seconds, she waved a thick stack of cards, all containing the exact information Karen had prayed for. "I meant to throw those away days ago, but something kept me from doing it."

In the clutter of the mail room, the four of us celebrated this surprising answer to prayer.

On the surface, Karen's request appeared trivial, but her friends knew otherwise. The young woman faced deep, wrenching turmoil in her life. Her prayer answer offered warm affirmation of God's presence with her. Before long, Karen took courageous steps to secure help with her difficult situation. She knew God was listening.

Are you excited about prayer? Or do you think that breathtaking answers disappeared ages ago? If you are willing to pray, get ready to see God work through your ministry of specific prayer.

Specific prayer has taught me to bring people, events, and concerns to the Lord in a vital, personal way. I have learned that as I pray *about* these definite requests, allowing God to decide what is best, I am overwhelmed by His loving replies.

If you want to experience dynamic, life-changing answers to prayer, learning how to pray specifically can launch you into a tremendous adventure with God. This book can show you how to revolutionize your prayers and your faith as you witness God's power in your life. If you are willing to trust God, if you have an interest in others, a notebook, some time each day, and a thankful heart, then you are ready for a ministry of specific prayer. And this book will help you get started. Here are some of the things you will learn:

> The guidelines for specific prayer.
> How to design and use a prayer notebook.
> How to make specific requests.
> How to respond to prayer answers.
> Creative ways to pray.

Each lesson presents a key step in establishing a prayer ministry. Principles give fundamental truths about specific prayer. Anecdotes demonstrate how these principles work.

Some special features enhance the use of the handbook. The "Memory Verse" introduces a Bible verse that adds greater knowledge and appreciation of prayer. You might want to make a copy of the memory verse on a 3" x 5" card and memorize and apply the verse during the week. Scriptures are taken from the New International Version. "Questions for Discussion" are provided to encourage serious reflection and application to the individual reader as well as lively interaction between students involved in a group study. The "Assignment" at the end of the lesson helps the reader/student to make application of the principles and brings the message into his life.

The last section of the book contains helps for the teacher who wants to lead a group of students into a prayer ministry. Special features are included to maximize the learning experience. The "Lesson Aim" clearly defines what you want to accomplish in the lives of the students as a result of the lesson. "Materials Needed" tells what supplies are needed for the meeting. "Learning Goals" chart the course for the lesson, indicating the smaller goals that will be reached in order to achieve the overall "Lesson Aim." Finally, the "Session Strategy" gives step-by-step plans for conducting the session.

In this age of advanced technology, we often miss the greatest communication system in the universe. Prayer is the believer's direct line to God. Through specific prayer, we can experience God's personal love and concern. Learning how to pray specifically is a gift you can give yourself and others. That is the purpose of this book.

I'm sure you will find, as I have, this investment brings far reaching rewards.

Accept the Challenge

Get It in Gear!

Each week when I was a young teen, I used to catch a ride to prayer meeting with our neighbor, Willy Gustafson. I was too young to drive, and Willy enjoyed company on his trips to midweek service. So each week, he started his old car and rumbled down the road. "Here comes Willy!" I would yell; then I'd grab my Bible and off we'd go to church.

Willy didn't shift gears after he stopped to pick me up. He always drove in low gear. After I jumped in, we'd try to carry on a conversation. "Any sweet corn yet?" I'd shout.

"Nope!" he'd holler back. "How's your dad's pigs doin'?" The next three miles, we yelled at each other, trying to talk over the roar of the hard-working engine.

Prayer without direction can be similar to Willy's struggling, overworked automobile. The necessary components are present for smooth operation, but the driver, the one praying, is unfamiliar with how much more power is available.

For instance, when we arrived at our meeting, many requests were "unspoken." Several folks regularly stated, "I have an unspoken request." Being a curious sort, my imagination ranged far and wide trying to pin down what mysteries we might be winging toward Heaven that evening.

When we did verbalize our requests, many of us prayed for generalities. "Bless the missionaries." "Go with our loved ones." "Be with the unsaved; You know who they are." "Thanks for Your many blessings." "Guide us through this week."

We didn't feel the excitement of tiptoeing into God's presence, whispering our deepest joys and longings in His ear. Because of this, we missed receiving clear-cut answers, life-changing proof of God's personal involvement in our lives.

Perhaps my childhood years sparked my desire to talk more directly with God. My parents thought their family was complete before I arrived. But they welcomed me as a bonus, not as the burden of another child to raise. My dad, a hard-working painter, often lifted me onto his lap after supper for a heart-to-heart talk.

"What did you do today, Lenie?" he asked. He let me comb his hair in ridiculous styles as we laughed and shared stories. The best part of this lap sitting was the closeness I felt as I talked with my father.

When I became God's child, I realized He also wanted me to climb up in His lap and talk things over with Him. He accepted me with full rights and privileges. He welcomed my visits with open arms. He wanted me to receive direction, affirmation, and love gifts from His generous heart.

My problem was—I didn't know how to pray.

A New Approach to Prayer

Years later, a Bible study group showed me a way to shift my requests from low gear into drive. The rules, which were already set, drew me like a magnet:

- Avoid unspoken requests.
- Make specific requests that allow you to see direct, visible results when God answers.
- If you pray about physical needs, ask for the answer to increase faith, change attitudes, and glorify God in addition to meeting the physical need.

What difference did this new type of prayer make? We started to see results! As we prayed about specific aspects of the requests, we began to receive answers. Of course, not every prayer was answered "yes." Sometimes an emphatic "no" came, or "wait." We learned that God's *nos* and *waits* were answers, too! The startling reward was the close, personal relationship our group gained with God through prayer.

Since then, I have used this form of prayer with groups of various ages and with my family. Praying for specific petitions does not replace praise, confession, and thanksgiving. Instead, specific prayer enhances those times spent with the Lord.

Questions to Consider

1. How do you compare your present prayer life with Willy's car, being driven in low gear?

_____

_____

2. What difference do you think following the three rules for specific prayer might make in your prayer life?

_____

_____

3. How can receiving a "no" or a "wait a while" increase your faith?

_____

_____

4. How do you think "specific prayer" might enhance prayers of praise, confession, and thanksgiving?

_____

_____

Benefits of Specific Prayer

If you want a fresh look at God's power, consider these benefits found in a ministry of specific prayer.

• **Specific prayer invites you to communicate with God about every detail of your own life and of those for whom you pray.**

"Can you look at my manuscript on prayer?" I asked my friend the other day. Leslie is an accomplished writer. I can always trust her editing skill to catch my mistakes. But that time we disagreed. Across from my sample prayer list, Leslie wrote, "Sounds like a 'to do' list to me."

In many ways, specific prayer incorporates the "to do" lists of life. I enjoy asking God's direction about an idea for a devotional, a solution for a computer snarl, or the wisest time to fly to an ailing parent's side.

In Sue Monk Kidd's book, *God's Joyful Surprise,* she quotes Madeleine L'Engle's thoughts on bringing God into the core of our lives: "There is nothing so secular that it cannot be sacred." Specific prayer allows discussion of the most ordinary details with God.

•Specific prayer welcomes God, seeks His will, and talks things over with Him. It helps you to align your will with His, to accept what He answers with a thankful heart.

My daughter Mary entered the world looking for adventure and has made the most out of every minute since. I often wondered whether we would both survive her trip to adulthood. We did.

I have prayed as Mary canoed down the Amazon, backpacked in Alaska, and visited the Maasai people in Africa. Even her profession is daring. She directs paramedics by radio and leads trauma teams in a large medical center.

Recently, Mary asked me to pray with her about a decision. A position was opening in a different field. Qualified applicants were being sought. "What shall I do, Mom? Shall I try for it?"

We listed the gains and losses she might expect with this change. The opportunity looked exceptional for a young person. However, other factors tempered the glow of the offer. We asked God to make His plans for Mary evident through the panel who would choose the person for the position.

When the answer came, we felt assured and happy. Mary knew the result was God's best for her.

•Specific prayer shows others that God is actively involved in the lives of those who trust Him.

Lynn sat across from me in a lay counseling session last spring. She looked dismally sad as we discussed her recent breakup of a long relationship. "Can you describe your feelings about God in the midst of this crisis?" I asked.

Scanning the room, Lynn's eyes focused on the top of the high bookcase behind me. She pointed to a small figurine, barely visible over the edge. "He feels like that. Distant. Cold. He's out there somewhere, but He doesn't care about me."

"I'm glad you can be so honest with your feelings, Lynn," I said. "Have you ever told God how far away He feels to you?" As Lynn and I continued to talk, I told her some of the difficulties I had faced during the past year. "Only God's personal touch kept me going in the dark places," I told her.

"Why don't you ask God to make himself evident in your life?" I challenged.

Lynn promised to pray specifically for a sense of God's presence. And she kept her word. Three months later, we met for lunch. She talked nonstop. She was seeing a new friend. She was taking college classes. She had started a different job. She radiated joy.

"How do you feel about God now?" I asked.

Poking the table with one finger, Lynn laughed, "He is right here with me. When I began asking Him to reveal himself in the everyday activities of my life, He did! I have never felt this closeness before."

Questions to Consider

1. Which of the three benefits of specific prayer (listed above) do you find the most exciting? Why?

_____

_____

2. In what definite ways could these benefits help you during the week ahead?

_____

_____

3. Do you agree or disagree with the statement quoted above: "There is nothing so secular that it cannot be sacred"? Why?

_____

_____

4. Do you think others can tell "God is actively involved" in your life? How do you think you might demonstrate this more clearly?

_____

_____

Specific Prayer: A Transferable Concept

Specific prayer can do these same things for you. You can watch God move in the midst of your appointments, conversations, and concerns. You can witness dramatic changes in your attitude or, perhaps, in the response of someone else. And you can share the good news that God still listens to and answers prayer. You will learn how to do this in the lessons to follow.

Memory Verse: Psalm 5:3

"In the morning, O Lord, you hear my voice; in the morning I lay my requests before you and wait in expectation."

Assignments

1. Read Psalm 5:3. Write five requests to pray about this week. Make a commitment to wait in expectation for the answers.

2. If you are using this study in a group setting, pray every day for each person in your group. Ask God to hear and respond to these new adventurers in prayer. Also pray enthusiastically for the five requests that you recorded.

Check the Guidelines

Little Blessings

"We want to be farmers again!" my husband's parents said. As retirement neared, nostalgic memories of country life beckoned to them. Soon they had sold their home across the bay from San Francisco. They bought ten undeveloped acres east of Sacramento and settled into a mobile home to enjoy their retirement. But three years later, the frog pond no longer sounded musical, and a drought had turned their oasis into an oven. Mom and Pop yearned for city life again. They began to prepare their dream for sale.

We expected them to face difficulties in selling the isolated farm. I decided to ask God to send a buyer. I talked to Him about it every day for four months.

On Thanksgiving Day, Pop announced, "We're going to list the place with a realtor on Tuesday." While contacting a realtor was the logical business decision, I had asked God to surprise us in the way the farm sold. The hard work required by the acreage had exacted a heavy toll on both parents. They needed affirmation of God's care.

"What are You going to do, Lord?" I prayed. "I can hardly wait to see."

On Monday, a man driving along the main highway a mile from the site made a right turn onto the deserted road that passed in front of the acreage. With no "For Sale" sign or other hint of the property's being available, the stranger drove his car up the rough quarter-mile driveway and parked by the mobile home.

"Would you by any chance be interested in selling this place?" he asked Pop, who was hoeing nearby. As they talked, my father-in-law learned that this buyer was genuinely interested in the property. He wanted the mobile home. He wanted the portable sheds. He even wanted the garden tiller. And he paid cash for the entire purchase! God had provided a fresh start on a new future.

In September, 1988, Mom and Pop celebrated their sixtieth wedding anniversary. I prayed for months for their health problems to stabilize so they could enjoy this momentous event. God answered. A canopy of joy covered the entire weekend.

Times aren't easy for them these days. But Pop still serves Communion, and Mom supervises a bit at the church rummage sales. The requests I prayed for them may sound trivial, but they were important to many people around my husband's parents. God never told us to bring only the big things to Him. He wants to give us both big and little blessings.

Take a Look at Scripture

Specific prayer is Scriptural. This is not some new innovation. The following principles are based on Scripture, yet these are only a few of many that could be cited. You can be confident that this concept is true to the Scriptures.

Jesus Instructs Us to Bring Needs to Him

Ask and it will be given to you; seek and you will find; knock and the door will be opened to you. For everyone who asks receives; he who seeks finds; and to him who knocks, the door will be opened (Luke 11:9, 10).

Jesus tenderly met needs. He comforted a sorrowing mother. He visited with an extortionist. He touched a person with a communicable disease. Jesus notices and cares about our longings. He asks us to bring them to Him in prayer.

Jesus Provides a Way for Us to Come Confidently to God

> For we do not have a high priest who is unable to sympathize with our weaknesses, but we have one who has been tempted in every way, just as we are—yet was without sin. Let us then approach the throne of grace with confidence, so that we may receive mercy and find grace to help us in our time of need (Hebrews 4:15, 16).

Roy and Ebba co-hosted a small group with my husband and me one year. They were the first people we knew who lived in a gated community. When our group met at their home, I loved driving up to the guard at the luxurious complex.

"What are your names and who are you visiting?" he'd ask.

"Jack and Darlene and we're here to see Roy and Ebba!" we would answer.

After a quick call over the intercom, the guard replied, "They're expecting you!" He smiled and waved his welcome to the private community.

Jesus invites us to meet with Him in a far better place than a gated community. He died to give us the right to be part of His family. We who know Him as Savior are accepted in the Beloved. He welcomes us into the holy of holies in prayer.

Paul Taught the Necessity of Praying Specific Requests

> And pray in the Spirit on all occasions with all kinds of prayers and requests. With this in mind, be alert and always keep on praying for all the saints (Ephesians 6:18).

Through example and word, Paul taught specific prayer—for oneself and for others. His own prayer list was long. He prayed diligently for churches, leaders, and new believers. His workload grew daily. Persecutors dogged his footsteps. So he prayed. And he taught others to pray, also.

How did Paul ever find time to pray? Paul apparently knew the prime importance of prayer. The busier he became, the more he needed to pray for himself and those serving with him.

On a much smaller scale, I once had two hundred teenagers, all new believers, in my prayer notebook. The burden of caring for this great number of new babies in Christ overwhelmed me. I felt compelled to pray for them. Paul's example and his fruitful ministry were my guiding light.

Questions to Consider

1. Which of the principles from Luke 11:9 and 10, Hebrews 4:15 and 16, and Ephesians 6:18 do you find most relevant to your needs this week? Why?

   _____

   _____

2. Read Psalm 141:2. What does this verse suggest about making our prayers acceptable to God?

   _____

   _____

Take a Look at Your Spiritual Life

Before you enter a ministry of specific prayer, take some time to consider the standards God requires of those who seriously pray. First John 5:3 says, "This is love for

God: to obey his commands. And his commands are not burdensome." As you read the following guidelines, you will find they are "not burdensome." Does your life align with them? Or could you use a few changes before you begin?

Make Sure You Belong to God's Family

If you feel doubtful about your faith, ask your minister to show you the Bible's message of salvation. If you have accepted Jesus as your Lord and Savior, you need not doubt your relationship (1 John 5:13-15). Thank God for His gift of salvation. If you have not, then you need to do so.

Believe God Counts You Worthy to Pray

Do you question whether the discussion of specific requests with God might be presumptuous? When I feel that way, I take a fresh look at my position in Christ. Paul says, "And God raised us up with Christ and seated us with him in the heavenly realms in Christ Jesus, in order that in the coming ages he might show the incomparable riches of his grace, expressed in his kindness to us in Christ Jesus" (Ephesians 2:6). This verse gives God's grace as the basis for our welcome into His presence. Grace makes it possible, through Christ.

Confess Sin and Accept Forgiveness

Do your best to keep your relationship with God free from attitudes and activities that grieve Him. Psalm 66:18 says, "If I had cherished sin in my heart, the Lord would not have listened." But since most of us slip up in many ways, we need the promise of 1 John 1:9, which says our confession of sin brings full forgiveness. The only step remaining is to forgive ourselves.

Take a Look at Your Attitude

David Seamands, in his book, *Putting Away Childish Things*, writes profound guidelines on prayer. He includes three that are absolutely vital.

God Does Not Violate Human Freedom

As you pray specifically for others, you may pray about hurting relationships, abusive bosses, and unsaved friends. Remember that God created each person with a free will to make his own choices. While God's desire may be the same as yours in a situation, He will not overstep the other person's free choice.

Give God the Timing for the Answer

God's timing, like everything else about Him, is flawless. We often get impatient, but God knows just when to act for the best advantage, just as He did in sending His Son "when the time had fully come" (Galatians 4:4).

I often look back on answers that seemed to take a long time in coming. Sometimes I find the answer came at a much better time than when I first asked. In fact, the timing sometimes proves to be as much an affirmation of God's care as the answer itself.

Pray Childlike, Not Childish, Requests

Prayer is a transaction between a mature believer and the Creator of the universe. Be thoughtful in your requests. Seamands closes his chapter on prayer with a reminder that God always answers prayer, and He does it either by changing the circumstances or by supplying power to overcome them. "He answers either the petition or the person." Understanding this helps us move to maturity in prayer. Our interest, Seamands says, "is no longer the gift, but the Giver."

Questions to Consider

1. Read the principles under "Check Your Spiritual Life" and "Check Your Attitude." Which of these causes you the most trouble or anxiety? What steps can you take to resolve this problem?

   _____

   _____

2. Name some practical ways the guidelines under "Check Your Attitude" can help as you pray.

   _____

   _____

   _____

3. How is giving God the timing for answered prayer similar to allowing God to change the person (you) instead of—or as well as—the petition?

   _____

   _____

4. How would you rate your own maturity in prayer? How can you become more mature?

   _____

   _____

Memory Verse: Psalm 141:2

"May my prayer be set before you like incense; may the lifting up of my hands be like the evening sacrifice."

Assignment

Write a letter to God. Tell Him in clear, concise statements why you believe you are prepared to pray. Continue praying for your five requests.

Start a Prayer Notebook

Benjie

Benjie was a teenaged orphan who accepted Christ in an outreach group Jack and I sponsored. He needed a home, and he soon found one with a family whose daughter attended our church. Benjie required extra patience and many prayers. He tended to be irresponsible.

Many times, Benjie telephoned to say, "Mrs. H., I want to take my driving test today. Can you go along?"

Of course, Benjie wanted my car, not me. Before Benjie won his coveted driver's license, Benjie, my car, and I had made seven trips to the Department of Motor Vehicles!

That was several years ago. Since then, Benjie has served in the armed forces and has earned a master's degree. Last summer, he invited us to his wedding. He now ministers to several hundred teenagers as a youth pastor.

Like Benjie, the people in your prayer notebook can become stars in the drama of life, no matter how unlikely that seems now. You will cry with them and cheer for them. They may be the folks next door or your Aunt Mable in Colorado. However, when you begin to pray, amazing things happen. I assure you, few other ventures could bring greater happiness and fulfillment.

How to Make Your Own Prayer Notebook

This lesson contains the simple steps to making a prayer notebook. It includes information on the type of notebook to use, how to choose people to include on your list, how to gather requests, and how to format the names and requests on the page.

Choose a Notebook

You can use any type of notebook, but a loose-leaf binder is best. This will give you the freedom to add pages or rearrange pages if you need to. Choose a simple, inexpensive binder that will hold standard notebook paper, usually 8 1/2" x 11", ruled, with three holes for the binder. Choose between wide and narrow ruled paper according to your own preference and writing style.

Decide for Whom You Will Pray

Whom will you place on your first specific prayer list? You may already have a prayer list that you follow regularly. If so, write these names in your notebook. (You will learn how to pray specifically for them in a later lesson.)

A prayer list may be a new concept to you. A good way to begin is to write your name on the top line. Next, add the names of people whom you love and care about most. Then add those who are part of your regular activities. Since you are involved in the lives of these individuals, you can pray specifically for them. You can also keep in touch more easily to see how God is working through your prayers. You may want to pray for the following people or groups of people:

Your Immediate Family
Your mate and your children
Parents, brothers, and sisters

Your Extended Family
Aunts, uncles, and grandparents
Nieces, nephews, and grandchildren

People Who Share Your Ministry
Sunday-school class
Youth group
Support group

Your Spiritual Leaders
Missionaries
Pastors and their families
Sunday-school teacher

Others
Neighbors
Close friends
Your roommate
Co-workers
Your boss

Begin with a small group of people. You can add others later. If you start with too many names, you may get discouraged and give up!

Gather Specific Requests

After you write the names for your first prayer list, the next step is to learn what to pray for each one. Use these principles as a guide.

Learn How to Listen

Let's face it. Most of us hear plenty of prayer requests, but we forget to listen. We let the other person's words slide by in order to get to the important things: what we want to say. A key factor in learning specific requests is simply to pay attention when you are conversing with others.

Ask Questions

You can learn many requests by asking family members and friends about their schedules and activities. Asking, "What's happening in your life this month?" may yield many topics for prayer. Are they presenting a project at work? Is their church seeking to buy land? Are they celebrating, anticipating, or recuperating? Most people are overjoyed to find someone to share the happy and sad times in their lives through prayer.

Cultivate Awareness

In addition to listening and asking for requests, just keep your eyes open. A hidden need may show up in the form of a sad face, a flat voice, or a drooping posture. Be aware and take time to learn how others genuinely feel. When you ask, "How are you?" a person may say, "I'm fine," but all the while his nonverbal message is saying, "I hurt. Will you pray for me?"

Record Requests

When you do hear a specific request, record it. Carry a pad of paper with you. If you don't have writing material, write the request on the back of your checkbook. Or, if all else fails, write it on the palm of your hand. You won't forget to record that request in your notebook!

Learn to Integrate Emotional, Physical and Spiritual Needs

While a person's greatest need is to know God, emotional and physical needs must sometimes be met first. Here are a few examples of this from my own prayer notebook:

A man reeling from a divorce needed to rent a small room where he could begin to heal after the separation from his family.

Two girls taking a long motor trip around the United States needed to make calm, wise decisions if emergencies arose.

A researcher needed ideas in developing diagnostic tools for a rampant disease.

One of the most unusual requests I ever prayed was for a watermelon in December. Long before produce was shipped in from sunny climates, I asked God to help me find a watermelon for a wedding dinner. I looked everywhere, but none could be found.

The day before the wedding, three watermelons showed up in the market a mile from my home. The produce man, shaking his head in disbelief, said, "Never saw that before, never expect to see it again. Came in this morning on a truck from Texas!"

The physical need sounds superficial, but God's personal gift to a young couple's wedding left a profound impression. Don't forget, Christ's first miracle occurred as He supplied refreshments for a wedding.

Become Known as a Person Who Can Keep a Confidence

Some requests, such as the watermelon, give everyone a cause to celebrate. Many requests—maybe most of them—are too personal to allow out of the strictest confidence. Learn to talk only to God about matters that cannot be shared. When requests go no further, folks will know you are a trustworthy prayer partner.

Become Known as a Person Who Believes in Prayer

The church kitchen was filled with mouth-watering aromas one October evening. Crystal punch bowls and autumn flowers added to the tables set for the grand event. Our pastor's alma mater was holding an annual meeting at our facility. Nothing had been spared to make this a memorable occasion.

About an hour before the dinner, we began questioning the aroma from the pork roasting in the ovens. Could it be spoiled? Quickly, we took some of the meat and dashed to the butcher shop. The owner confirmed our fears. The pork could not be served.

Without a minute to spare, we gathered in a circle to pray. Our pastor joined us. "Lord, you fed five thousand with five loaves and two fish. Will you help us feed a crowd of hungry people right now?" he asked.

When his "Amen" sounded, someone shouted, "Kentucky Fried Chicken! We have several stores nearby."

Phones rang at each franchise. Cars raced out from the parking lot. Every available piece of Kentucky Fried Chicken within miles winged its way toward our church.

The meal, with a divinely provided entree, reached the tables thirty-five minutes after we prayed. The guests cheered. We became known as women who believed in prayer.

Questions to Consider

1. Consider each of the suggestions for gathering requests. On which do you need the most improvement? What can you do to improve in this area?

_____

_____

2. Have you taken time to listen to someone this week? If so, what did you learn?

_____

_____

3. Did you record a prayer request this week? What method did you use?

_____

_____

4. Jesus integrated emotional and physical needs with spiritual needs. Name two or three examples of emotional and physical needs of people you know, and how your prayer for these needs might result in spiritual rewards.

_____

_____

_____

5. Why is keeping a confidence vital in a prayer ministry?

_____

_____

Start Your Notebook

The following steps show you a simple way to make your own prayer notebook. Use a sheet of paper to make a trial copy of your first month's prayer list.
1. Write the month and year across the top of the page.
2. Begin at the left side. Write your name on the first line. Leave room for requests beside your name.
3. Add names down the side of the page, using at least one line for each name. Begin with people closest to you. Leave room for requests beside each name.
4. Begin thinking about requests to add for each person next week.

Try to rewrite your list each month. Because specific prayer often deals with current activities, many requests are answered quickly. Beginning each month will also give room to add new requests as you receive them. Usually, when people discover someone who prays, requests arrive regularly. A third reason to start over each month is to gain a sense of growing anticipation for future events. A wedding, a graduation, or a home purchase may go through many stages of planning and preparation. However, when the day arrives, you will know your faithful prayers helped bring the hope to reality. Finally, since the arrival time of some answers will be indefinite, rewriting the requests each month allows you to make a fresh commitment to pray for each concern.

Sample Prayer List

Myself
Daily Bible reading and prayer.
Relaxing vacation (June 10-17).
Ideas for Jill's wedding reception.
Doctor's appointment (June 28).
Walk two miles a day.
"Encouragement day" with Grandma.
Learn a lot at discipleship seminar

First Child:
Great birthday party.
Find missing music sheets.
Get necessary classes for fall.
Learn from and enjoy youth group
    trip to orphanage.
Right job for summer

Spouse
Meet project deadline June 30.
Enjoy racquetball tournament.
Great anniversary weekend.
Talk with [child's name] about
    [problem].
Resolve differences with [co-worker].

Neighbors:
All come to block picnic.
Nancy's surgery.
New job for Joe.
Healing of the Moores' marriage
    problems.
Break from the kids for Jenny.

Second Child

Find reason for reading difficulty.
Safe flight to Grandparents' house.
Enjoy helping with VBS.
Fun with friends at party June 20.

Parents:

Mom's blood pressure lower.
Dad drive safely to the airport.
Enjoy [grandchild's] visit.
Get acquainted with new minister.

Sunday-school Class:

Ryan: find a way to make him smile.
Kevin: help him quit punching (and
    learn *why* he punches).
Chris: a good visit with his mother.
Brad: write him a note for helping.
For entire class:
    Better attention.
    See response.
    Set date for pizza party.

Ask God to Empower Your Prayer Ministry

After reading this lesson, you know how to gather requests. You have learned that praying for emotional and physical needs can give opportunities to meet spiritual needs. You are aware that your love for people and prayer can welcome others to trust you with their concerns. Now, ask God to empower your ministry. The adventure is about to begin.

Questions to Consider

1. List the names of several people whom you wish to include in your prayer requests. Then write beside each name a definite way that your prayers might enhance each person's life.

_____

_____

_____

_____

_____

2. How might answers to your prayers for them enrich their faith? How might such answers enrich your own faith?

_____

_____

_____

3. What four reasons are given to make a new list each month? How do you think this will help you?

_____

_____

_____

_____

4. Look at the sample prayer list. Do any of the requests surprise you? Why? Can you think of a reason these might have been included?

_____

_____

_____

Memory Verse: James 5:16

"The prayer of a righteous man [or woman] is powerful and effective."

Assignment

Begin your own prayer notebook. Write this week's theme verse, James 5:16b, at the top left-hand side of the page. Add the month and the year. List the names of those for whom you will pray. Pray for the names on your list each day.

Make Specific Requests

Lunch at Tijuana

Jack and I sponsored a college group that crowded into a small room for Bible study each Wednesday night. Every inch of floor space was filled. Even the stairway leading to the upstairs offices was packed with young people for our meetings.

One night, as we discussed our weekend outreach trip, Jack announced, "Most of you are on tight budgets, but give what you can for the lunch we're taking to the orphanage. The kids always act happy with a change from rice and beans."

Students passed a basket around the room. They tossed in one-dollar bills and change and then returned the offering to me.

When we arrived home, I counted thirty-five dollars and seventy-two cents. I prayed, "Lord, we have to feed sixty-five orphans and thirty-five of us. You and I need to do some talking about that lunch for next Saturday!"

I asked God to be my partner in the project. We discussed some specific details:

"Please show me how to stretch the money."

"What can I serve?"

"Where shall I go shopping?"

"Lord, my veteran cookie sheets are still on active duty!"

"Will you go to the market with me on Friday?"

And He answered every question.

When I entered the market, I found hot dogs, nearing their expiration date, marked to an unbelievably low price. The rolls were on sale, and yesterday's baking was half price. Even the catsup, mustard, and onions were reduced in cost.

I added chocolate chip cookie ingredients, potato chips, and drink mix to the shopping cart. When I checked out, the clerk shook his head, "Thirty-five dollars and seventy-two cents—for all of that?"

We enjoyed a magnificent day at the Tijuana orphanage.

Sharpen Your Focus

As you write your prayer requests, ask God to help you make them specific. State the activity, the need, the hurt, or the goal connected with the request. Add dates or descriptions to help you add focus to the prayer. What do you, or the person for whom you are praying, want to see God do? State the desire on the line following the person's name.

Look at the suggestions that follow. Choose from these or come up with your own. These are only suggestions to get you started.

Suggestions for Praying for Yourself

Pray that you will be open to God's Word and His plans for you.

Pray that your life will reflect Jesus.

Pray that you will complete work on job assignments or home projects. (List the specific project you are trying to complete.)

Pray that you will plan for and enjoy your guests on a special occasion coming up. (List the names of the guests and the occasion for their visit.)

Pray for creative ideas for the use of your leisure time.

Pray for ideas for a program for which you are responsible, or for a gift for a friend or family member (especially if a special day is near), or for a letter you need to write.

Pray that you will discipline yourself in some area. List the specific physical, emotional, or spiritual concerns you have.

Pray for courage to talk with someone (one of your children, a friend, or a neighbor, for example) about something that has been bothering you. Again, list specifically the person's name and the issue that needs to be discussed, such as a misunderstanding, problem behavior, or the person's faith.

Pray that you will be a better (or more relaxed) organizer.

Pray for a balance between your life at home and at work.

Pray that you will enjoy holiday preparations.

Pray for help in finding a new home or church.

Pray that you will feel the proper response to a child still at home, leaving home, away from home, or returning home.

Suggestions for Praying for Your Mate or Roommate

Pray that the person will have closer communication with God, with you, and/or with the children.

Pray for safety in travel.

Pray for healing of a problem (state it specifically and the desired resolution) with an employer or employees.

Pray for ideas, solutions, and/or progress on a project at home or at work. (Identify the project on your list.)

Pray for help in building a team spirit in a specific family, sports, church, or civic activity.

Pray that the person will receive affirmation of his or her worth through work, the church, the family, or neighbors. (If there is a particular area where the person's self-worth is especially threatened, pray about that, too.)

Pray that the person will take care of himself physically, emotionally, and/or spiritually. Note the particular area that is most likely to be ignored.

Pray for a happy, restful vacation.

Pray for health concerns.

Pray for successful ways to cope with stress.

Pray for peace during transitions of life.

Pray for joy and blessing in church responsibilities.

Suggestions for Praying for an Individual Who Is Sick

Pray for response to treatment.

Pray for pleasant rapport with medical personnel.

Pray for a positive attitude.

Pray for proper rest.

Pray for encouragement and hope.

Pray for the correct amount of visitors: not too few or too many.

Pray for a sense God's closeness.

Pray for strength for those who care for the patient.

Pray that God will be glorified through the experience.

Suggestions for Praying for Missionaries

Pray for energy.

Pray for patience.

Pray for acceptance of culture differences.

Pray for fluency in the new language.

Pray that homesickness will be alleviated.

Pray for the children's adjustments on the field and on furlough.

Pray for support levels to be sufficient.

Pray for response in ministry.

Suggestions for Praying for Your Pastor

Pray for encouragement from the congregation.
Pray for continued spiritual growth.
Pray for staff team spirit.
Pray for congregational unity.
Pray for time with family members.
Pray for message ideas.
Pray for a close confidante and prayer partner.

Suggestions for Praying for Students

Pray for good study habits.
Pray for a wise career choice.
Pray for a helpful advisor.
Pray for a job that integrates with school and church schedules.
Pray that financial needs will be met.
Pray for a close friend.
Pray for a sense of God's guidance.

Suggestions for Praying for an Engaged or Married Couple

Pray they may resolve or accept differences.
Pray they will talk with each other daily.
Pray they will keep growing emotionally, intellectually, and spiritually.
Pray they will take time for fun.
Pray they will see each other as a gift from God.
Pray they will encourage, praise, affirm each other.
Pray they will agree to spend wisely.
Pray they will learn to confront conflicts positively.

Suggestions for Praying for Hospitality in Your Home

Pray for a willingness to share your home with others.
Pray that you may view uninvited guests as divine appointments.
Pray that you will lovingly prepare for invited guests.
Pray that you will plan carefully.
Pray that you can enjoy the party, also.
Pray for preparation of your heart as well as your home.
Pray that the Holy Spirit may fill each room with joy.

Suggestions for Praying for Vacationers

Pray for safety in travel.
Pray for pleasant weather or successful coping with weather conditions.
Pray for good health during the trip.
Pray for friendly people and new adventures on the trip.
Pray for vacation expectations to be met or exceeded.
Pray for God to be welcomed in all areas of the trip.

Suggestions for Praying for Work Relationships

(These requests may be made for yourself in your own work, or they may be for someone else, perhaps a co-worker, a family member, or a friend.)
Pray to be known as a thoughtful, helpful, hard worker.
Pray to be pleasant and flexible with others.

Pray to be known as a team player.
Pray to live a balanced witness to co-workers (1 Peter 3:15).

Suggestions for Praying for Financial Needs

Pray for assurance that God knows your needs.
Pray that you will know how to make money stretch.
Pray for contentment with what you have.
Pray for God to answer your need in His way.

Suggestions for Praying for Spiritual Needs

Pray for consistent Bible study and prayer.
Pray for discipline in attitude and actions.
Pray for an awareness of God's presence.
Pray for a thankful heart for God's provision.
Pray for a prayer partner or support group to hold you accountable.

Suggestions for Praying for Problem Relationships

Pray for openness by both parties to discuss differences.
Pray for willingness to say "I'm sorry."
Pray for a mutual desire to find a workable solution.
Pray for eyes of love to see beyond the problem.

Suggestions for Praying for a Wedding or Other Celebration

Pray for direction in choosing the place, order of events, flowers, menu, music, and the guest list.
Pray for arrangements for out of town guests.
Pray for harmony among family and/or stepfamily members.
Pray for a canopy of joy over the entire occasion.

Ask Yourself

As you add requests beside each name for whom you have chosen to pray, ask yourself these questions:
• Am I willing to accept God's will in the outcome?
• Am I praying only to obtain *answers,* rather than have these *answers* used to accomplish a greater work?
• Can this request result in eternal value; can it encourage, affirm, or strengthen someone's faith?
• Can this answer bring glory to God?

Questions to Consider

1. Suggest some ways you can turn each of the following general requests into a focused request. Some help is given on the first one to get you started.

   • General: "Lord, bless all the missionaries."

   Focused: "Lord, be with _____, who is serving on the mission field

   of _____. Help him to get the _____ that he needs to continue his work."

•General: "Be with those who are sick and need Thy care."

Focused: _____

_____

•General: "Help me handle my money better."

Focused: _____

_____

•General: "Be with our church and the leaders of the church."

Focused: _____

_____

2. Read the Deuteronomy 3:24. Write three statements about God that you can claim for your specific prayer ministry. Which of these means the most to you? Why?

_____

_____

_____

3. What was the most surprising aspect about the suggested requests in the lesson? What did you learn from this aspect?

_____

_____

_____

4. Read the questions under "Ask Yourself." Why is it important to accept God's will, even if you wanted a different answer?

_____

_____

5. How could an answer for a physical or emotional need being met bring eternal value?

_____

_____

6. How could an answer to a prayer about a small detail in your life bring glory to God?

_____

_____

7. In what ways do these questions provide a safeguard on your prayers?

_____

_____

You Are Ready to Begin

As you begin your prayer notebook, consider this *your* personal venture with God. Make your book as creative and unique as *you* like. You may add requests for each person throughout the month. You can also add pages if you meet other individuals or hear of other needs to place in your notebook.

Each month will be a new beginning. This is your first step on an exciting journey. Let God lead you into new, uncharted territory!

Memory Verse: Deuteronomy 3:24

"O Sovereign Lord, you have begun to show to your servant your greatness and your strong hand. For what god is there in heaven or on earth who can do the deeds and mighty works you do?"

Assignment

Read this week's memory verse every day before you pray for your specific requests. Remind yourself that God himself is acting on your behalf.

Begin Your Adventure

Open Our Eyes, Lord

"Who is the traitor among us?" roared the king of Syria. "Who is telling the king of Israel what I plan? Find the culprit and bring him to me!"

Of course, we can only imagine the real conversation between the king of Syria and his servants. The event is recorded in 2 Kings 6:8-23, where we read that the king of Syria suspected a spy among his own troops because the king of Israel always knew where the Syrians were planning to strike. He must surely have been outraged, ready to exact blood as the price for treason. "Who is the traitor?" he wanted to know.

"None of us, my lord the king," said one of his officers, "but Elisha, the prophet who is in Israel, tells the king of Israel the very words you speak in your bedroom" (verse 12).

The king retaliated by sending a great army against Elisha. When Elisha's servant saw masses of soldiers and horses circling the city, he was terrified. "What shall we do?" he cried.

Elisha spoke first to his servant. "Don't be afraid," he said. "Those who are with us are more than those who are with them." Then he talked to God: "O Lord, open his eyes so he may see."

"Then the Lord opened the servant's eyes, and he looked and saw the hills full of horses and chariots of fire all around Elisha" (verses 16, 17).

Do you need a reminder of God's unseen presence? Specific prayer can open *your* eyes to the presence of God within you and power of God around you. He will move dramatically through your prayers, if you ask.

Your prayer notebook is ready. You have a list of individuals for whom you will pray and some requests to pray for them. Now, you can begin. Here are some hints to help you.

Make Prayer Times Count

•Make Prayer a Priority in Your Schedule

Give prayer an important place in your day. Make a commitment to bring these requests to God in consistent, daily prayer. While you may sometimes miss your prayer time, try to pray regularly. If you promise to pray for someone, do your best to follow through with your commitment.

•Choose Your Best Time

Some people wake up ready for action. Others don't really get going until the middle of the day. Still others come alive at night. Choose the hour when you feel you are at your best, a time when when you can escape from the busyness of your life for your appointment with the Lord.

•Don't Get Stuck in a Rut

Try new, refreshing approaches to your prayer time. Sing a hymn or praise song occasionally. You don't have to sing well or loudly. God has good ears and, I trust, transposes sincere praise into angelic song.

Change the order of your prayer list from time to time. Instead of praying for yourself and those closest to you first, begin with requests at the bottom of the list. This will help you avoid memorizing requests until they become almost meaningless repetition.

• Take Prayer Seriously

Although specific prayer often brings refreshing, delightful answers, remember you are carrying out a serious transaction between you and God.

• Approach Prayer as an Exciting Adventure

Habakkuk 2:1 says, "I will stand at my watch and station myself on the ramparts; I will look to see what he will say to me. . . ." Be willing to stand on tiptoe, expectantly waiting for God's reply.

• Use Your Bible

Prayer is a dialogue, so read your Bible as part of your prayer time. You can find models for prayer, answers to prayer, and encouragement to pray in God's Word. Since Scriptures are timeless and prayer is precious to God, you may hear Him speak directly to you through His Word.

Another way to make Bible study especially meaningful before prayer is to record a three-way version of each verse in a short passage.

First: Ask, "What does the verse say?"
(Write the verse exactly as it appears in Scripture.)
Second: Ask, "What does it mean?"
(Paraphrase the verse in your own words.)
Third: Ask, "How can I use this today?"
(Write a practical way to make the verse part of your day.)

• Remember to Say Thanks

When answers come, circle them boldly. A circle signifies completion. You can also add exclamations, happy faces, or personal thanks along the page. Choose your own way to celebrate and be grateful. On the last day of the month, spend your prayer time thanking God for His answers.

Late one night, the ringing telephone woke me from a deep sleep. "Hello," I answered sleepily.

A frantic voice on the other end of the line cried, "Mark's in the hospital! We just brought him to the emergency room in terrible pain. Will you please pray?"

Mark was a newcomer to the high-school youth group that Jack and I sponsored. His mother had also started attending our church, and we had met briefly. "Of course, we'll pray," I said. And we did.

The next day, I drove to the hospital to check on our young friend. His mother rose to greet me in his room. Laughing nervously, she wrung her hands and said, "Oh, I am so sorry I called you. Mark only had appendicitis. His surgery went perfectly. You really didn't need to pray!"

"Didn't need to pray"? Of course, we needed to pray! And God answered our prayers. But how easily we assume that doctors and hospitals and everything else except God are responsible for the outcome of certain situations. Yet God is there. He has promised to be involved. He has promised to answer prayer. And He keeps His promises. Don't forget to thank Him.

What to Do if a Request Remains Unanswered

Don't become discouraged if you don't receive an answer immediately. When God says "no" or "wait," ask Him to show you whether to keep on praying about the situation. Perhaps the time is not right for the answer to be given. Or God may send something better at a later time. He may also be teaching you deep truths that you can learn only by trusting Him without knowing the outcome.

If the answer is "wait," transfer the concern to the next month in your prayer notebook. Make the request part of your continuing adventure with God.

You may enjoy calling some of the people on your prayer list to see whether they received an answer as you prayed. Ask them if they want you to continue to pray about the matter. Recently, I called someone whom I had met briefly at a convention several months earlier. I had promised to pray for her. But as her phone rang, I thought, "Will she even remember me?"

"Of course, I remember you!" she said. And, as we talked, she shared how God had provided far beyond what we had agreed to ask Him for in her life.

Questions to Consider

1. List three ways you can make your prayer time more meaningful.

_____

_____

_____

2. How do you plan to follow these?

_____

_____

3. How can your Bible be a useful part of your prayer time?

_____

_____

4. Why do you think we often forget to say thank you?

_____

_____

Creative Ways to Pray

"Look up there!" the wedding guests cried out as they pointed skyward one summer day near the beach. Weddings occur often on that bluff overlooking the ocean. But this wedding was different. The groom had added a special touch of his own.

High above us, a small plane trailed a huge sign, "I love you, Stacy!" The bride threw herself into her new husband's arms and kissed him. The crowd cheered. The bridegroom had found a creative way to communicate his love.

Prayer, our communication with God, thrives on newness, innovation, freshness, and creativity. You may think of many more ways to pray than I suggest here. Use these as catalysts, your booster rockets to send you soaring into greater heights of creative prayer.

•Personalize Scripture

The Gospels contain numerous verses to use in your personal conversations with Jesus. One of my favorite Scriptures tells about Mary, Martha, and Lazarus, who enjoyed a close friendship with Jesus. He loved their family and visited often in their home.

Mary, Martha, and Lazarus encountered many of the same problems that contemporary families face. They disagreed about priorities. Household duties became cumbersome at times. And, when a crisis occurred, their only hope was running to Jesus for help. When Lazarus became very ill, for example, "the sisters sent word to Jesus, 'Lord, the one you love is sick'" (John 11:3). I have been amazed to see the surprising, faith-building answers to prayers when my family and I personalize this verse.

Some time ago, I prayed, "Lord, Mary, whom you love, needs a house." With escalating housing prices, she faced a major challenge. But prayer, coupled with many extra overtime hours and a diligent search, helped Mary find the place she now happily calls home.

Recently I prayed, "Lord, Jeanne, whom you love, is trying to get into a university media production program." The program was closed. Every class in the department was filled. But then, almost miraculously, the doors opened. Jeanne is a full-time media production student.

•Pray Scripture Back to God

There are dozens of passages of Scripture that are really prayers or God's words to His children. Take one of these Scriptures and make it your own prayer. A couple of examples are shown below to illustrate the concept.

Example 1:
Scripture (Psalm 57:2): "I cry out to God Most High, to God, who fulfills his purpose for me."

Prayer: "Lord, I cry out to you about this transition our family is making. You have promised to fulfill your purpose for us in this move to Toledo. Guide us to the neighborhood, the schools, the church, and the friendships where we can carry out your plans for our future. In Jesus' name, amen."

Example 2:
Scripture (Isaiah 49:16): "See, I have engraved you on the palms of my hands."

Prayer: "Lord, I thank you for writing my name on Your hand. Please remind me that You are thinking of me as I give my report to the committee today. In Jesus' name, amen." (Note: Make a mark on your hand to remind you of God's care.)

Sometimes, a verse of Scripture will reveal the prayer of someone in behalf of another. Paul, for example, frequently told the people to whom he wrote that he was praying for them, and what it was he was requesting from God. Use these verses to pray for someone you love. Put his or her name and any specific application into the prayer.

Example:
"I pray that out of [Your] glorious riches [You] may strengthen [the person for whom you are praying] with power through [Your] Spirit in [her] inner being, so that [You] may dwell in [her heart] through faith" in [describe the present situation] (Ephesians 3:16, 17).

•Claim a Scripture Promise

Don't be bashful about claiming the promises recorded in Scripture that have universal application to all Christians. Claim these promises for yourself and others—and be creative about it!

Example 1:

Philippians 4:19 says, "And my God will meet all your needs according to his glorious riches in Christ Jesus." Claim that promise for yourself or a friend by making out a check:

	March 23, 1990
Pay to the Order of: ____*Jennifer Barnett*____	$ *Confidence*
____*Confidence in solo part of "Mr. Mean Strikes Out!"*____	
God's Bank Account Philippians 4:19	____*Christ Jesus*____

Example 2:

Personalize Jeremiah 32:27 with a prayer like this: "Lord, I know You are the Lord, the God of all mankind. Nothing is too hard for You. I believe that, in Your chosen way, You can [state what you need God to help you do].

•Pray for Making Triumph Out of Troubles

When facing a difficult situation, pray this prayer, substituting the person and/or problem that you are facing:

"Lord, I believe that You can use [name the situation] to lead me into deeper knowledge of You or greater use for You. Show me what I can learn about You from this. How can I serve You through this?"

•Pray for Someone Who Is Rejecting Christ's Love—and Perhaps Yours

I cannot speak to you of God
Since so wise you grew.
My one recourse, in love, is this,
To speak with God of you.
                    Author unknown

•Pray for Help in Finding Your Destination

Do you ever get lost? I do.

Jesus knew the disciples needed help to find the place where they could observe Passover with Him. This meal would become the last supper. He told them to look for a man with a jar of water who would direct them to the place.

"So he sent two of his disciples, telling them, "Go into the city, and a man carrying a jar of water will meet you. Follow him" (Mark 14:13). The "man with the jar of water" showed them the way to the upper room. They found the room furnished and ready for the significant meeting before the crucifixion.

God has helped me, a person who gets lost quite easily, in some unusual and delightful ways. When I couldn't find my way to a travel service in heavy Southern California traffic, I prayed, "Lord, I need a 'man with a jar of water.'" Suddenly a large tour bus with my exact destination on it guided me right to the door of my appointment. Another example happened a few weeks ago. My friend and I were late to pick up an editor at the airport. We could see planes flying in, but the entrance to the terminal eluded us. I prayed and immediately we saw a city street worker, setting up his day's project. "Can you tell us how to get into the Ontario airport?" I asked. He became our 'man with a jar of water,' as he explained how to reach the airport in a few minutes.

Creative Times to Pray

When you become familiar with the specific requests on your prayer list, you can pray for them virtually any time. Here are just a few suggestions:

While you wait at traffic signals.
While you stand in lines at the post office, bank, or supermarket.
While you wait for appointments.
While you walk, drive, or fly.

Remember: You can pray during any activity in which you might converse with a beloved friend. That is what prayer is!

Questions to Consider

1. Which of the "Creative Ways to Pray" appeals to you most? Why?

_____

_____

2. Do you think all Scripture verses can be personalized, or all promises claimed? If not, how do you decide which ones can?

_____

_____

3. Read John 12:20-22. How might you personalize verse 21?

_____

_____

4. What additional "Creative Times to Pray" can you add to the list above?

_____

_____

Put Feet on Your Prayers

As you pray for specific needs, you may become aware that you are able to help answers come to pass. For instance, Kate, a member of our Bible study group, was battling a difficult illness. We put feet on our prayers by collecting dozens of upbeat cards and letters that expressed how much Kate meant to us. We pasted the sentiments into a scrapbook and sent the gift as a visible expression of our concern.

Adding feet to prayers may also be accomplished through connecting two requests on your prayer list. You may be unable to remedy the situation yourself. However, you may see how both requests may be answered if the individuals meet each other.

About ten years ago, Jim and Marty became permanently disabled. Unable to work, each needed an encourager, prayer partner, and friend. As I prayed, I saw the similarity of their life circumstances. Soon after they were introduced, Jim and Marty began meeting together. Since then, their partnership has endured some tough times, but their friendship continues to thrive. They talk regularly on the phone and seldom miss their biweekly visits to each other's homes.

The most dramatic answer I have seen to putting feet on a prayer happened with my favorite college teacher, Mr. Long. Mr. Long extended a hand of mercy to me as a returning student. I walked into his crowded graphics art lab on the first day of class with a look that must have screamed, "Help!"

I was terrified about going back to school. A mistake on my registration required me to add this class. I could see there was no room. Every desk was filled. Students stood along the walls.

Mr. Long said, "Come back tomorrow. I'll find a place for you."

Because of him, I found courage to return.

During the school year, I learned Mr. Long was facing a bitter disappointment. He was nearing retirement age, but needed to work one more year to make his future secure. The school hierarchy sent him a notice saying he must retire—immediately.

Sensing his sadness, several of us asked, "What can we do to help?"

"You could write letters during the summer to the college president. Tell him I'm still a good teacher," he suggested.

Mr. Long was not only a good teacher. He was the best I would ever have. He arrived promptly each class time, prepared, enthusiastic, and equipped with years of experience in the commercial art field. On top of that, he showed genuine interest in each of his students.

During the summer, everyone else apparently got busy and forgot to write. My prayer list kept reminding me. I sent one *extremely specific* letter to the college president, and prayed many *specific* prayers to God.

That fall, Mr. Long came back. He showed me his letter from the college board. The letter said that he could stay. My letter was attached to it. Because of one letter and those prayers, Mr. Long could teach two more years.

Several other students and I set to work. All year we sorted through stacks of Mr. Long's years of artwork. We organized a one-man art show. We held a reception. We served hundreds of cookies that had been baked and donated by students across the campus. Enthusiasm swept across the school about our new celebrity.

The benefit of the art show was twofold. Students were delighted to own some of the popular teacher's work. We also accumulated a substantial amount of money for him as well.

When retirement time arrived, honors poured in. Mr. Long was named the first professor emeritus. He received full rights and privileges to all college facilities. He was honored in the paper, across campus, and in his classes.

When the school celebrated an anniversary two years later, Mr. Long was named one of the most significant people in the history of the college. All of this well-deserved recognition came because some feet were added to a prayer.

God has unique tasks for you to carry out. You can help people whom no one else may reach. Ask for creativity from the One who designed the universe. Make footprints for God's glory.

Here are some suggestions of ways you can put feet on your prayers:

Supply a needed baby-sitter.
Connect two lonely people.
Write a letter of recommendation.
Organize a scrapbook of encouragement.
Save a person's job.
Form a missionary booster club.
Supply or secure transportation.
Cook a double meal to share.
Send a happy-face cake or pizza.

Remember: God may be waiting on you so He can answer a prayer in an amazing and wonderful way!

Questions to Consider

1. What do you think about putting feet on your prayers?

_____

_____

2. Can you recall a time when you put feet to your prayers? If so, what happened?

_____

_____

Memory Verse: Habakkuk 3:2

"Lord, I have heard of your fame; I stand in awe of your deeds, O Lord. Renew them in our day, in our time make them known."

Assignment

1. Choose two of the creative ways to pray and use them throughout the day.

   Methods chosen: _____

   _____

2. Pray for the requests in your prayer notebook daily.
3. Put feet to at least one request this week.

Celebrate the Results

Off to School

Sherrie dashed excitedly into the house, waving a letter. "I'm accepted!" she called out as she ran through the rooms, looking for someone to share her news.

Pride and sadness collided as I realized that our firstborn was going away to graduate school. The University of California in San Diego, only a hundred miles away from our home, sounded far away.

"We'll ask God to find you just the right roommate," I said, as I hugged her my congratulations. Right away we began to pray for just the right person to share her apartment with her.

The school soon sent out questionnaires to help students find suitable roommates. Questions ranged from "Do you smoke, have a pet, like loud music, or have a religious affiliation?" to "Do you clean your room once a week, once a month, or when you move?" As Sherrie completed the forms, she cautiously wrote, "Yes" to "Do you have a religious affiliation?" She knew "religion" might mean many different things at a secular university.

We prayed diligently about her future roommate. We asked for someone compatible, who could become a genuine friend, and who might share her field of studies. We added, "And please, God, could you also send a believer?"

One day, a letter arrived from Seattle. Joyce Tamashiro, who sounded as shy as my daughter, was interested in further correspondence. "Are you a Christian?" she included in her letter. Sherrie wrote back, affirming that she was. Joyce answered quickly. She, too, was a Christian!

Looking back to that event ten years later, we realize how God's provision exceeded our requests. Both Sherrol and Joyce played the guitar. They shared similar church backgrounds. They preferred quiet surroundings. They were even memorizing the same Scripture, Psalm 139. The crowning touch came several months later when they entered the same graduate lab to do virology research.

Sherrie and Joyce shared the apartment for two years before Sherrol married her college sweetheart. However, the girls spent a grueling seven years together in the graduate program. In fact, the ordeal became so difficult that they might never have completed the program without the support and encouragement they received from each other. They received their doctorates in 1985.

Sherrie is now a molecular biologist, performing pioneer work in the genetic sequencing field. Her present research focuses on the development of a genetic probe to help screen the AIDS virus from the nation's blood supply.

Joyce is married and lives in Seattle, Washington. She teaches biology at a private university. Though separated by distance, the girls' friendship remains close.

Rewards of Specific Prayer

Sherrie and Joyce's story demonstrates the wide variety of benefits gained through specific prayer. You can claim these principles for your prayer ministry. Note how they held true for us as we prayed.

•Specific prayer colors your prayer life with anticipation and excitement.

We could hardly wait to see who Sherrie's roommate would be. God's choice was better than we thought possible.

•It shows God's power in both the large and small aspects of life.

God placed these young women in the same laboratory, even though there were many laboratories in the large university. God provided that each owned and brought household items the other did not bring, even down to muffin tins.

•It keeps your relationship with God current as you pray daily.

God gave each of the girls a prayer partner, to meet together for support and encouragement on an ongoing basis.

•It provides strength to help you survive difficult times.

God supplied a custom-designed confidante and friend for the endless hours of research.

•It encourages you to completely trust this personal God you love.

God placed two shy young women in a group of scientists who did not acknowledge Him, yet kept their faith strong and true. God turned their years of research into the exact training for the jobs awaiting them upon graduation.

Questions to Consider

1. The incident described above demonstrates God's interest in our concerns. Do you need His attention to get you through some crisis or to make a major decision? Write the details of your request.

   _____

   _____

2. Read 2 Chronicles 6:9. What idea in this verse means the most to you? Why?

   _____

   _____

3. How do you think these "Rewards of Specific Prayer" can enhance your own life? Include physical, emotional, and spiritual aspects.

   _____

   _____

   _____

4. Have you been using specific prayer since you began to use this handbook? If so, what rewards have you found?

   _____

   _____

   _____

Other Rewards of Specific Prayer

• It helps you feel at home with God.

When I was about five years old, Emil and Winnie often asked me to go home with them after church. Their own children were grown, and my elderly grandparents were unable to care for a young child, so all three of us benefited from the arrangement. I treasure my memories of the many cozy hours spent in their home.

"Let's read the Bible," Winnie would say. Their remotely situated home had no electricity, so we gathered by the glow of her kerosene lamp. Winnie skillfully skipped over many words because she couldn't pronounce them. I didn't care.ITThe feeling of being at home with God permeated Winnie's home, her life, and her words. She lived every moment with the Lord.

When you become accustomed to specific prayer, God's presence settles in, as He did in Winnie's home. Jesus said, "If anyone loves me, he will obey my teaching. My Father will love him, and we will come to him and make our home with him" (John 14:23). The word for "make our home with" in this verse conveys the warmth of living in close union with God, an intimacy that is ours with God through His Son Jesus.

The natural, everyday type of conversations found in specific prayer builds a feeling of being "at home." Add the clear-cut answers received as you pray specifically, and you will find assurance of your intimate partnership with God.

• Specific prayer can free you from fear.

Fear rushes in from many sources these days. I received calls about two newborns this month. Both babies struggled with breathing difficulties. The future loomed uncertainly. Their parents needed prayer for freedom from fear.

A young couple's marriage has faltered for three years and has now crashed into divorce. All efforts to help save the marriage failed. The wife struggles to care for their four small children. We are praying together for freedom from fear.

Psalm 34:4 says "I sought the Lord, and he answered me; he delivered me from all my fears." While the outcome of these cases is still unknown, we know two things. First, we know that fear does not come from God (Romans 8:15; 1 John 4:15-18) Second, we know that because these believers have asked, God is supplying a "peace that passes all comprehension" (Philippians 4:7).

• Specific prayer unleashes God's power in your life.

> Now to him who is able to do immeasurably more than all we ask or imagine, according to his power that is at work within us . . . (Ephesians 3:20).

Each Sunday, police officers direct the traffic outside of my church. When the officers blow their whistles and hold up their right hands, rows of cars brake to an abrupt halt. Another whistle and a wave starts the opposing traffic moving ahead.

The power does not come from the officers. They could not stop a single car with their hands. The ability to regulate tons of automotive strength lies in the authority given to them by a higher power. In traffic control, the authority comes from the police department and the state in which the officer works.

Your authority in prayer also comes from a higher source: God himself. As you come humbly before Him, not looking for glory for yourself, He can release His power through you.

• Specific prayer can encourage new faith or restore waning faith.

> You were shown these things so that you might know that the Lord is God; besides him there is no other (Deuteronomy 4:35).

Answer me, O Lord, answer me, so these people will know that you, O Lord, are God, and that you are turning their hearts back again (1 Kings 18:37).

Sometimes, the only way to reach people is to pray for them. You can't preach at them. You can't tell them how wrong and hopeless they are. But, you can show them that God answers prayer. Be interested in those around you. Learn their concerns. Pray for them. You may celebrate their new trust in God as they see answers to your prayers on their behalf.

• Specific prayer produces a joy-filled heart.

You have filled my heart with greater joy than when their grain and new wine abound (Psalm 4:7).

My friend Mary is the incarnation of a joy-filled heart. I met Mary when she and her husband accepted Christ after an evening service. Since then, Mary's faith has flourished. Her life, which had always overflowed with good deeds, now shines with the strength of the Lord. She works full-time as a teacher's aide, yet she carries on a giant ministry to others. Mary maintains a phone list to encourage others. She sends out notes. She volunteers with a hot line each week. Her husband survived cancer against great odds a few years ago. Now Mary works with a cancer support group to help those still in the battle.

Most important of all, Mary prays. I know that at 5:30 A.M., she is praying for me and my family. She accomplishes marvelous works for God through prayer.

Last summer, Mary had a serious surgery. My sister and I went to visit her. We joined a crowd of well-wishers who waited for a chance to express their love. Inside, Mary's room was lined with tall racks, each shelf laden with floral arrangements and plants. Her joy-filled life of prayer has touched hundreds of lives.

• Specific prayer teaches you to hang on in the bad times.

But if I go to the east, he is not there; if I go to the west, I do not find him. When he is at work in the north, I do not see him; when he turns to the south, I catch no glimpse of him. But he knows the way that I take; when he has tested me, I will come forth as gold (Job 23:8-10).

Life is not all sunshine and birthday parties. A friend may die. A job may end. A child may rebel. No matter how sincerely you pray about some requests, the answer may not bring your heart's desire. However, if you have experienced God's personal touch in the past, you can trust Him to guide your future.

• Specific prayer allows you a glimpse of the sovereignty of God in your life.

O Lord, you are my God; I will exalt you and praise your name, for in perfect faithfulness you have done marvelous things, things planned long ago (Isaiah 25:1).

"The longer I live, the more I appreciate the sovereignty of God," Jim said. "You know, God's sovereignty almost means as much to me as God's love."

I agreed. Jim and I were discussing past events as we waited for our lay counselor's supervision meeting to begin. Our friendship extends back over fifteen years. We knew that God had shown us "perfect faithfulness." He had "done marvelous things." And He was still working out His plans in our lives.

For instance, specific prayer has shown me God's sovereignty on a personal level. In answer to prayer, God gave us a neighborhood that has become family to us. Teachers contributed imagination and knowledge to our children. Youth work brought bright young people to inspire all of us and to make us keep growing.

Specific prayer has shown me God's sovereignty in the lives of others for whom I have prayed. I see how God has led a group of young women who were seeking direction. Lisa became a neonatal nurse. Marie is a pastor's wife. Janis shares an international ministry with her husband.

God's sovereignty need not take dramatic turns to be significant. He has supplied a baby-sitter, a needed postage stamp, or a happy song on the radio right when I needed them.

The sovereignty of God has placed me where I can share my love for Him. For instance, nine years ago, Jack and I made a call for the visitation-evangelism team on which we served. Cassie, a young woman in her twenties, opened the door.

After talking with us awhile, Cassie invited Christ into her life. Before we left, our new friend took a photograph of us holding a large Bible to send to her family in the Midwest.

"They'll never believe this without a picture," she said laughingly.

Last month, we were invited to a small gathering to celebrate Cassie's dedication to Christ. She has continued to grow because God sent another couple to nurture her in the faith.

Cassie hugged me tightly and said, "My life was in such chaos when you came and told me about Jesus. Thank you so much for coming."

I believe God's sovereignty sent us there.

Questions to Consider

1. The author says specific prayer can make you feel "at home" with God. How is a warm, loving home environment like a warm, loving prayer time?

_____

_____

_____

2. How is specific prayer a good cure for fear?

_____

_____

3. How do the promises of Psalm 34:4, Romans 8:15, and 1 John 4:15-18 help you engage in your ministry of prayer without fear? Write one anti-fear, pro-faith statement that could be put on a banner to encourage you (or others).

_____

_____

4. Read through the "Other Rewards of Specific Prayer." How can these make your life happier, richer, and more meaningful?

_____

_____

_____

_____

Memory Verse: 2 Chronicles 16:9

"For the eyes of the Lord range throughout the earth to strengthen those whose hearts are fully committed to him."

Assignments

1. Pray daily for the requests in your prayer notebook.

2. Add new requests as you hear about them.

3. Notice the circled requests—the ones that have been answered—and praise God.

Where Do You Go From Here?

Now What?

As you complete this study, you may be asking, "What do I do now? I'm enthused about praying, but I need direction on how to keep this momentum going."

Specific prayer can be your private, quiet labor of love. However, God may challenge you to multiply your efforts and spread the excitement to your entire church. Whether you choose to pray alone or with a group, the following suggestions can help you to continue on with your prayer ministry.

Keep a Record

The lessons in this book give you simple, humble ways to pray. The ideas work because you learn how to talk with God about genuine concerns for yourself and others. You also keep a journal of His faithfulness. As you write requests and note when answers come, you can see how much interaction takes place between you and your Heavenly Father.

Take Time to Grow

A specific prayer ministry needs time to mature. Allow several months to discover your own unique style. Gather requests in ways that suit your life-style and personality. Let your prayer notebook show your creative handiwork. Select a time in your schedule when you can concentrate best. This is your ministry, to be designed and carried out as God directs you.

Cultivate a Relationship

A successful prayer ministry requires the same principles as a good marriage or other close personal relationship. The long-term results depend on your willingness to invest in the project. Note how your attitude can determine the quality of your relationship with God through prayer:
1. You can skim over the surface in polite conversation, or *you can share the deepest longings in your heart.*
2. You can soon grow bored with the whole idea and take your partner for granted, or *you can bring fresh, vital creativity into your mission.*
3. You can bail out when you receive your first big disappointment, or *you can build a trust that grows deeper each year.*
4. You can consider your time spent making a notebook, gathering requests, and praying as drudgery, carried out with a sense of duty, or *you can welcome prayer as a privilege, a loving relationship between you and God.*

Take a Fresh Look

If you need an occasional brush-up course on this study, find help quickly by reviewing the topics covered in each lesson:

Lesson One at a Glance

Find a Scriptural, creative way to pray specifically.
Talk to God about details of your life and of others.
Welcome God into your plans.
Align your will with His.

Accept results with a thankful heart.
Acknowledge God's active involvement in your life.

Lesson Two at a Glance

Set guidelines for requests that honor God.
Find Scriptural support for specific prayer.
Prepare your heart to pray.
Keep your attitude pleasing to God.

Lesson Three at a Glance

Make a prayer notebook.
Assemble materials.
Choose names for your prayer list.
Gather requests.
Organize the notebook.

Lesson Four at a Glance

Make specific requests.
Ask yourself about the validity of these requests.
Follow suggestions for using your prayer notebook.

Lesson Five at a Glance

Make prayer a priority.
Make prayer times count.
Integrate Bible study with prayer.
Pray creatively.
Put feet on your prayers.

Lesson Six at a Glance

Realize how prayer can enhance your life.
Find benefits in everyday circumstances.
Enjoy lasting spiritual rewards.

Celebrate God's Faithfulness

One of the greatest gifts of learning to pray is the knowledge that you can always depend on God. Those who continue to pray acquire a strong affirmation of His care. In joy-filled times, you will marvel at God's great provision. In stormy days, He will hold you on a steady path.

Remember these verses:

Though the fig tree does not bud
   and there are no grapes on the vines,
though the olive crop fails
   and the fields produce no food,
though there are no sheep in the pen
   and no cattle in the stalls,
yet I will rejoice in the Lord,
   I will be joyful in God my Savior.
The Sovereign Lord is my strength;
   he makes my feet like the feet of a deer,
he enables me to go on the heights.
                              Habakkuk 3:17-19

Keep on Praying

"What a beautiful dining room!" I remarked as my friend took me on a tour through her home. Elegant draperies framed the windows. The furniture, made of polished woods, was carefully arranged. In the china cupboard, the finest crystal and china sparkled.

As we visited, I learned a sad truth about that dining room. No one ever ate there. The family's meals were served in the kitchen. When company came, they were taken to a restaurant. The exquisite dining room remained lifeless. It needed to be used to fulfill its purpose.

The methods and ideas in this book are like that dining room; to fulfill their purpose, they must be used. You can give them life. Open your heart to others. Learn their needs. Give yourself freely to prayer. Then watch God work in response to your requests.

Ideas for Groups

If you have used this study in a group, or want to begin doing so, consider these possibilities for the future.

Plan #1: Prayer Partners

As you complete Lesson 6, assign partners to keep in touch with each other by phone. Suggest that one partner call once a week or once a month to learn how the other partner is doing with his prayer notebook. Partners can take turns making calls. This can be especially helpful during a month when one person is finding answers scarce on his prayer list. Perhaps that individual's partner can lend extra encouragement and friendship during those times.

A call to a partner about a long-awaited or dramatic prayer answer will also strengthen this bond and increase faith.

Plan #2: Letter of Commitment

As you complete Lesson 6, give each person a slip of paper. Ask everyone to write the present date and his commitment to pray during the next six months—or whatever length of time the group chooses. Also, ask each one to address an envelope to himself and place the commitment inside. Then mail each person his letter at the end of the designated time as a reminder of this commitment.

Plan #3: Class Reunion

Select a date when your group will hold a reunion. Ask the members to bring their prayer notebooks to the meeting. Discuss these topics together:
a. Of all the answers you have received, what was the most encouraging? . . . surprising? . . . dramatic? . . . unusual? . . . practical?
b. In what ways has your concept of prayer changed?
c. Can you describe how specific prayer has increased your faith?
d. How can our group encourage you to continue praying?
   At the close of the meeting, set another date for your next reunion.

Plan #4: Form a Prayer Committee

1. Organize your group into an ongoing prayer committee.
2. Choose a regular meeting time and place.

3. Place an enthusiastic description of your prayer ministry in your church bulletin or newsletter. Include a phone number, inviting people to call you with their requests.

4. Invite your church staff, lay workers, and missionaries to submit current needs.

5. Use the guidelines in this study to put a sharp focus on requests.

6. Ask those who submit requests to call back when they receive answers.

Plan #5: Start a Churchwide Prayer Ministry

1. Place an invitation in the church bulletin or newsletter to everyone who wants to join your prayer ministry.

2. Schedule a sign-up table in the church foyer for several Sundays to gather names of those who want to be involved. Ask participants to give names, telephone numbers, and area codes.

3. List your phone number in the bulletin or newsletter for those who want to sign up by phone.

4. After sign-ups are complete, choose one of the following ways to organize your church prayer ministry:

Prayer Chain

a. Appoint a prayer leader whose phone number will appear regularly in the church bulletin and newsletter.

b. Provide each prayer chain member with a list of names and phone numbers of all prayer chain members.

c. When a request is called to the prayer leader, he will record the request in a notebook, adding the date. He will then phone the first person on the list. The leader will relay the request in a brief, accurate account. Prayer chain members will find that writing each request helps to relay the concern more correctly.

d. Each prayer chain member will pass the request along in the same manner, continuing until the last person on the list is reached.

e. Whenever a person cannot reach the next person on the list, he will call the one after that, continuing until someone receives the message. A request may be left on an answer machine. However, the caller must continue phoning until another member is reached. This ensures that the request will reach as many members as possible in the shortest amount of time.

f. Emphasize the importance of sincerely praying for the request immediately.

g. Callers who must skip names in order to find someone at home should call those people back later.

Prayer Teams

a. Appoint a prayer captain who will receive requests and pass them on.

b. Divide the names on the sign-up sheet into teams of five each. Assign a team leader for each team.

c. Give each leader the names and phone numbers of his team members.

d. Place the prayer captain's phone number each week in the church bulletin or newsletter.

e. When a request is called to the prayer captain, he will call each team leader with a brief and accurate account of the request. Each team leader will then call each member of his team, also giving a brief and accurate account of the request. Prayer teams may also function as mini-prayer chains, with each team using the prayer chain rules listed above.

f. Emphasize the importance of sincerely praying for requests as soon as possible.

Session Guide for Leaders
by Jonathan Underwood

Lesson One

Lesson Aim

The students should discover a Scriptural, innovative way to pray that allows them to see specific answers to prayer.

Materials Needed

Each student will need a Bible and a copy of this handbook.

Learning Goals

As a result of participating in this lesson, the students will do the following:
1. Define specific prayer.
2. List three "rules" for specific prayer.
3. Make a commitment to a ministry of specific prayer.

Session Strategy

Preparation

Have the students read *Get It in Gear!* Then divide the class into groups of three or four and have each group discuss the first question under *Questions to Consider* on page 8. Encourage the students to evaluate their own prayer lives. Are they struggling along, like a car in low gear, hardly getting anywhere? Or do they feel their prayers are effective, strengthening them and others in their ministries? If the former, can it be that their prayers are too general, like the examples cited in the lesson?

Ask the students to suggest one thing that they believe will improve their prayer lives. Allow each student to make one suggestion; then tell the class, "We're going to look at a new approach to prayer that may be just what many of us need."

Exploration

List the three "rules" for specific prayer on the chalkboard or on an overhead transparency. Then summarize the section entitled *A New Approach to Prayer.* Discuss each of the three rules together, asking the students to suggest how these rules can make their prayers more effective.

Then discuss the various ways God answers prayer. Point out that with specific prayer, God still answers "yes," "no," and "wait a while." But He seems to answer "yes" more often because we are really asking for something! James says, "You do not have because you do not ask God" (James 4:2), and that is precisely the problem with vague, general prayers. Specific prayer really asks, and God is true to His word to answer.

Finally, consider how specific prayer might be combined with prayers of praise, confession, and thanksgiving. Discuss how the concept can enhance these prayers as well. Each of these is more meaningful when we get specific. Brainstorm some specific praises that might be offered.

Application

Tell the class, "We've been talking about an approach to prayer that is probably new to most of us. We call it 'specific prayer,' but we've never stopped and stated just exactly what 'specific prayer' is." Ask for suggested definitions. Essentially, specific prayer is prayer that goes boldly to the throne of grace and just tells the Lord exactly what is on the mind of the one praying. It applies directly to petitions, asking specifically for what is desired, as well as to other types of prayer.

Ask the class, "What benefits do you think might be found from consistently praying in this manner?" After a few suggestions, have the class read *Benefits of Specific Prayer.* Return to the small groups and discuss the *Questions to Consider* that follow (page 10).

After a few minutes for discussion, get the attention of the entire class. Ask, "What do you think? Are you ready for a ministry of specific prayer?" Read the brief section, *Specific Prayer: A Transferable Concept.* Then ask the students to complete the assignments at the end of the lesson. Close with a prayer circle, encouraging the students to pray short, specific prayers.

Lesson Two

Lesson Aim

The students should learn how to establish guidelines for prayer requests that honor God and are acceptable to Him.

Materials Needed

Each student will need a Bible, a copy of this handbook, and a half sheet of paper.

Learning Goals

As a result of participating in this lesson, the students will do the following:
1. Cite Scriptural support for specific prayer.

2. List some principles for making their prayers acceptable to God.
3. Suggest some means of improving their spiritual maturity.

Session Strategy

Preparation

Read *Little Blessings*. Then ask the class, "Have you ever wanted something, but thought it was too trivial to talk to God about? What did you do?" Discuss this together, noting that God is concerned even about the seemingly insignificant aspects of life. Then ask, "If the apparent significance of a request is not the determining factor on how to pray, what kind of issues do you believe are involved in praying the right way?" After a brief discussion, tell the students that this lesson is designed to teach us some Scriptural principles for prayer.

Exploration

Draw three vertical lines on the chalkboard, making four columns. Write the following references over each one: Psalm 141:1; Luke 11:9, 10; Ephesians 6:18; Hebrews 4:14-16. Have the class read *Take a Look at Scripture* and then ask the students to suggest some principles for prayer from the passages cited. List each of these under the appropriate headings. Discuss these principles together: how difficult is it to follow them, what helps can be suggested, how can Christians support one another in them? Other questions might also be discussed relative to each principle.

Then move on to *Check Your Spiritual Life* and *Check Your Attitude*. Encourage discussion on these issues without prying. Use the *Questions to Consider* to stimulate the discussion, going beyond these questions into personal introspection as much as the class is willing to go.

Application

Pass out half sheets of paper (5 1/2" x 8 1/2") with a scale like the one shown below drawn near the top. Ask each student to mark the scale to indicate his or her own spiritual maturity level (0=not yet committed to the Lord; 10=perfect).

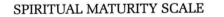

SPIRITUAL MATURITY SCALE

| 0 | 1 | 2 | 3 | 4 | 5 | 6 | 7 | 8 | 9 | 10 |

Ask each one to write below the scale what would be different in his or her life if the maturity level were one point higher. Discuss some of their ideas together, suggesting that they all choose one idea, whether their own or one they have heard in the discussion, and begin working on boosting their maturity.

Before closing the session, encourage the students to complete the assignment on page 14.

Lesson Three

Lesson Aim

The students should learn how to make a personal prayer notebook.

Materials Needed

Each student will need a Bible, a handbook, a three-ring binder, and ruled paper (8 1/2" x 11").

Learning Goals

As a result of participating in this lesson, the students will do the following:
1. Choose people for whom they want to pray.
2. List six principles for gathering requests.
3. Start a prayer notebook.

Session Strategy

Preparation

Read the story of *Benjie* on page 15. Ask the class, "Who is the most unlikely person you can think of who might someday be a significant leader in the church?" Some answers might be suggested aloud; many more will be thought but not spoken. Without comment on the ones suggested publicly, ask, "Is this person any more unlikely than was Benjie? Or Saul of Tarsus? What do you think would happen if you were to pray for this person every day consistently for a month? A year? Five years?"

Exploration

Each student should have a notebook for this lesson. If you are able to supply the notebooks for the class, that is great. More likely, you will have had to ask the students to get their own and bring them with them for this lesson.

Ask the students to look at the list of people under *Decide For Whom You Will Pray* on pages 15 and 16. Then have them open their notebooks and write the names of at least five people—one from each group—for whom they will pray. Stress that they are to use names, not the general titles listed in the handbook.

Then ask them to read *Gather Specific Requests*. When they have had a chance to read through this section, ask for a review of the suggestions, listing each one on the chalkboard or overhead transparency. Discuss them as needed to be sure everyone is clear on what is intended by each one. Then discuss the *Questions to Consider* on pages 17 and 18.

Application

Have the class read *Start your Notebook,* including the sample prayer list. Then discuss the *Questions to Consider* (pages 19 and 20). Spend just a brief time on this so you can get on to the *Assignment,* which is actually to begin their notebooks. Have them follow the instructions, adding names to the list they made earlier, if necessary, and then writing specific requests by each one.

After a few minutes, read *Ask God to Empower Your Prayer Ministry* and then close with prayer.

Lesson Four

Lesson Aim

The students should learn how to turn general requests into focused requests.

Materials Needed

Each student will need a Bible, a handbook, and his or her prayer notebook.

Learning Goals

As a result of participating in this lesson, the students will do the following:
1. Write three statements about God they can claim for their specific prayer ministries.
2. Practice changing general requests into specific ones.
3. List several specific requests in their prayer notebooks.

Session Strategy

Preparation

Ask two students to read Philippians 4:19 and Ephesians 3:20, 21. Then read *Lunch at Tijuana* and discuss how this incident illustrates God's extraordinary answers to prayer. Tell the class they can expect similar answers when they consistently pray specifically for their needs and for God's glory.

Exploration

Ask the students to look up Deuteronomy 3:24. Read the verse aloud; then ask the students to write three statements about God they can claim for their ministries of specific prayer. Suggest an example: "God has a 'strong hand' to do whatever it is we need to have done."

Divide the class into five small groups. Assign each group one of the following sets. Ask them to read the suggestions for praying for the people indicated and then write five specific requests for one or all of them. Each request should indicate clearly what is desired, for whom, when, and why. (Leave the "how" up to God!)

> Group 1: yourself and your mate (or roommate).
> Group 2: missionaries, pastor(s), and spiritual needs.
> Group 3: students, a married or engaged couple, and a problem relationship.
> Group 4: financial problems, sickness, and a work relationship (boss, employee, or co-worker).
> Group 5: someone on vacation, a wedding or other big event, and hospitality in your home.

Give the groups about ten to fifteen minutes to work on their requests. Then ask for the groups to report. Write one request from each group on the chalkboard. Or, if you have large sheets of newsprint, give each group one sheet and have them write their requests on the newsprint. They can display the sheets when they give their reports.

After all the groups have reported, call attention to the section, *Ask Yourself.* Review questions 3-7 under *Questions to Consider* on page 25. Then apply the questions to the requests listed earlier. Ask the class to suggest revisions as necessary.

Application

Ask the students to open their prayer notebooks and look at the names of the people for whom they wish to pray. Then have them list requests next to each name. Remind them to keep their requests specific (who, what, when, and why?) and to ask themselves the four questions on page 24.

Read *You Are Ready to Begin* and close with prayer.

Lesson Five

Lesson Aim

The students should learn to make prayer times count and to pray creatively throughout the day.

Materials Needed

Each student will need a Bible, a handbook, and a prayer notebook.

Learning Goals

As a result of participating in this lesson, the students will do the following:
1. List three ways to make their prayer times more meaningful.
2. Suggest at least one creative way to pray.
3. Plan a means of putting feet on their prayers.

Session Strategy

Preparation

As a class, sing the chorus "Open Our Eyes, Lord." Then ask a student to read 2 Kings 6:8-23. Remind the class that we don't need to see armies of angels to know God is with us. He will open our eyes when He answers our prayers. But that will not happen if our prayers are too vague or inconsistent. We have to make our prayer times count.

Exploration

Divide the class into four small groups. Tell each group it is to take two of the suggestions for making prayer times count (pages 27-29) and give two or three specific examples of each. Allow ten minutes; then ask for reports.

After the reports, discuss the *Questions to Consider* on page 29. (For number 1, choose three of all the suggestions from the reports.) After this discussion, allow time for the students to read the two sections, *Creative Ways to Pray* and *Creative Times to Pray*. Then discuss the *Questions to Consider* on page 32. During this discussion, be sure to warn the students about being too creative. Scriptures taken out of context can be grossly distorted—nor would you want to recommend anyone personalize the verse that says "Judas went out and hanged himself"!

Application

Read Joshua 7:1-13. Suggest one way to personalize verse 10 is to realize there is a time to pray and a time for action. Joshua was praying for victory when he should have been purging the camp. Sometimes God expects us to take action to accomplish the task instead of just praying.

That's the idea behind the section, *Put Feet to Your Prayers*. Have the class read that section and then discuss the *Questions to Consider*. Have the students suggest several ways of putting feet to their prayers in the coming week. Emphasize the *Assignment* and close with prayer.

Lesson Six

Lesson Aim

Students should discover how a believer's life can be happier, richer, and more meaningful through a ministry of specific prayer.

Materials Needed

Each student will need a Bible, a handbook, and a prayer notebook.

Learning Goals

As a result of participating in this lesson, the students will do the following:
1. List the rewards they have found in specific prayer.
2. Commit themselves to a continuing prayer ministry.

Session Strategy

Preparation

Read *Off to School* and then ask the students for their reaction. How does the story make them feel? Does it challenge them? Encourage them?

Move on to the *Rewards of Specific Prayer*. Note how these rewards came from both the praying and from seeing the answers. Discuss them further by using the *Questions to Consider* on page 36.

Exploration

It is hoped that your students will have been using specific prayer in their own prayer times by now. Ask them what benefits they have personally found in it. Share your own experiences and rewards, too. Then read *Other Rewards of Specific Prayer* and discuss how the students' and your experiences compare with what the author describes here. Discuss each reward individually, looking up the Scripture verse cited for each one. Then discuss the *Questions to Consider* on page 40.

Then look at the *Conclusion* (pages 41-44). Suggest that the students keep these handbooks someplace convenient and refer often to these pages as a reminder to pray. Review the suggestions on pages 41 and 42 together, concluding with an encouragement like, "Don't be like that elegant dining room—beautiful, exquisite, and lifeless! We are prepared for an exciting ministry of prayer. Don't let all we have learned go unused."

Application

Discuss the *Ideas for Groups* together. Choose one or more of them to continue your group's ministry of prayer.

Remind the students of the assignments on page 40. Close with prayer.